ROMEO & JULIET

PRESENTED BY

MICHAEL ROSEN
& JANE RAY

CANDLEWICK PRESS
CAMBRIDGE, MASSACHUSETTS

The Players

BENVOLIO
Montague's nephew

LORD MONTAGUE
Romeo's father

LADY MONTAGUE
Romeo's mother

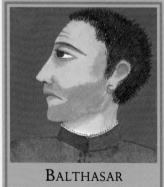

BALTHASAR
Romeo's servant

MERCUTIO
relative of the Prince

PRINCE
of Verona

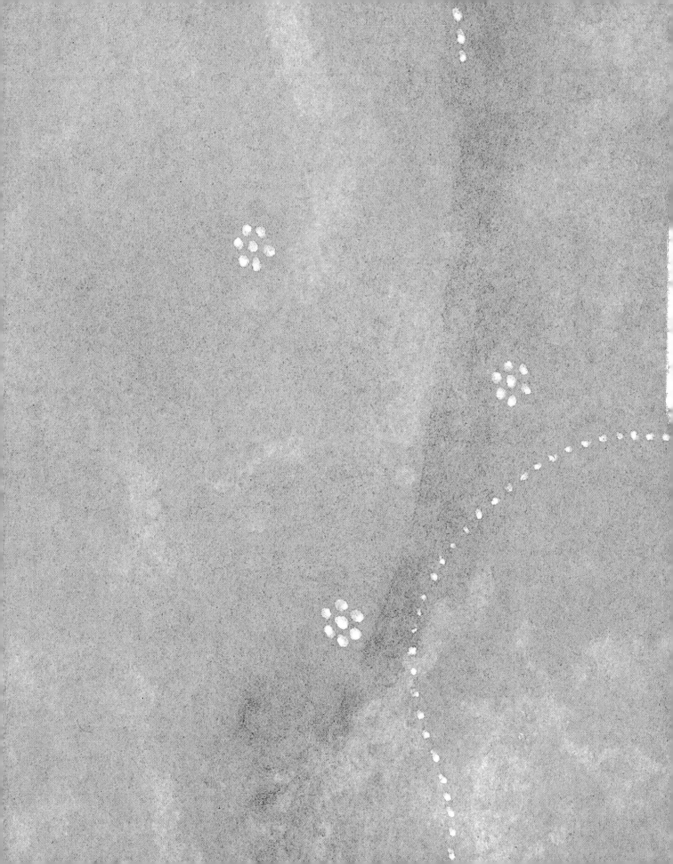

SHAKESPEARE'S

F*or Amelia Edwards* J. R.

Text copyright © 2004 by Michael Rosen
Illustrations copyright © 2004 by Jane Ray

First U.S. edition 2004

Library of Congress Cataloging-in-Publication Data is available.

Library of Congress Catalog Card Number 2003043836

ISBN 0-7636-2258-3

2 4 6 8 10 9 7 5 3 1

Printed in China

This book was typeset in Giovanni.
The illustrations were done in watercolor.

Candlewick Press
2067 Massachusetts Avenue
Cambridge, Massachusetts 02140

visit us at www.candlewick.com

LORD CAPULET
Juliet's father

LADY CAPULET
Juliet's mother

TYBALT
Lady Capulet's nephew

NURSE
to Juliet

7

COUNT PARIS
relative of the Prince

FRIAR LAURENCE
Franciscan friar

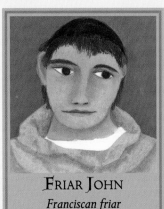

FRIAR JOHN
Franciscan friar

This is a story of one city, two families, and two lovers. It's a story that comes from a long time ago, a story that's been told many times in many languages. Some have told it in poetry, others in dance, song, and film. William Shakespeare told it in a London theatre in the 1590s. If you could travel now to that place and that time, you would find a London much, much smaller than capital cities today. It was a place of narrow, filthy streets, and houses made of wood and plaster, crammed full of people. Over it all towered a few buildings, including the Tower of London, with its torture chambers, prisons, and execution block, and St. Paul's Cathedral, full of singing, praying, incense, and ceremony. The 1590s were a time of great danger. England was at war, and many men were dying in

Ireland and the Low Countries. On the streets of London were people who knew how to kill and who had only just escaped being killed themselves. Some were hiding because they'd run away from the army. The wounded, who couldn't work, were also on the streets, begging. The plague wiped out hundreds of Londoners in those years. Many others died of hunger when cold winters made for bad harvests. So some people rioted in the streets. And in the countryside nearby, where the rich had put fences around the land to stop people from grazing their animals, angry groups of men and women tried to break them down. Meanwhile, in her court, Queen Elizabeth I herself was in danger. Some of the old noble families were secretly saying that they should rule the country, if not now, then after the old queen died. And other people who'd become rich in the last few years thought that they too should have a voice in how things were run. Queen Elizabeth and her advisers were ruthless with anyone who opposed them. They sent out spies, and their police imprisoned, tortured, and executed hundreds of people. In the midst of all this danger, something exciting was happening to the way ordinary people were entertained. There were new places to go where you could watch stories unfold in front of your eyes. You could see a power-hungry queen go mad, a cruel king kill a messenger for bringing bad news, a crowd of people rioting. One moment you might be watching a drunk staggering around making rude jokes, the next a sword fight, or a ghost reminding someone of terrible things done in the past. In these new places, people stood before an audience and told of their strongest feelings. They described how they were wildly, passionately, and unbearably in love; how they hated someone so much they wanted to destroy them; how desperate it was when you knew you should do something and could not summon the will to do it. . . . What was happening in these new places was— and is—the theatre. And it was in one of these theatres, in London in the 1590s, that William Shakespeare and a group of very ordinary men came together, looked at a poem called *The Tragical History of Romeus and Juliet,* and turned it into one of these amazing new entertainments.

First onto the stage stepped a storyteller. If, like many people then as now, you already knew the story of Romeo and Juliet, you might have expected the play to begin with the lovers. But no, it began with a picture of a rivalry between two of the top-ranking families of the city of Verona, the Montagues and the Capulets. It was a rivalry so great that it led to a kind of war on the streets, a civil war:

dignity: *social position*

mutiny: *violence*

> Two households both alike in dignity
> (In fair Verona, where we lay our scene)
> From ancient grudge break to new mutiny,
> Where civil blood makes civil hands unclean.

And then the storyteller told everyone the end of the story:

star-cross'd: *destined by the stars to have bad luck*
overthrows: *downfall*

> From forth the fatal loins of these two foes
> A pair of star-cross'd lovers take their life,
> Whose misadventur'd piteous overthrows
> Doth with their death bury their parents' strife.

Well, if we know how it's all going to turn out, then why hang around waiting to see what happens? Because, as Shakespeare and his friends understood, *how* it happens is the important thing.

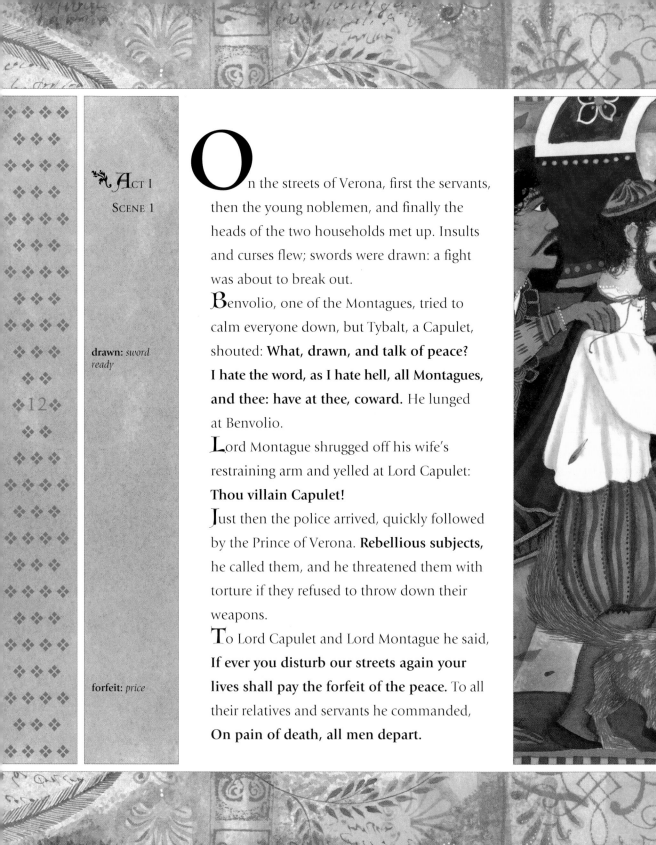

drawn: *sword ready*

On the streets of Verona, first the servants, then the young noblemen, and finally the heads of the two households met up. Insults and curses flew; swords were drawn: a fight was about to break out.

Benvolio, one of the Montagues, tried to calm everyone down, but Tybalt, a Capulet, shouted: **What, drawn, and talk of peace? I hate the word, as I hate hell, all Montagues, and thee: have at thee, coward.** He lunged at Benvolio.

Lord Montague shrugged off his wife's restraining arm and yelled at Lord Capulet: **Thou villain Capulet!**

Just then the police arrived, quickly followed by the Prince of Verona. **Rebellious subjects,** he called them, and he threatened them with torture if they refused to throw down their weapons.

To Lord Capulet and Lord Montague he said, **If ever you disturb our streets again your lives shall pay the forfeit of the peace.** To all their relatives and servants he commanded, **On pain of death, all men depart.**

forfeit: *price*

As the streets emptied, Lady Montague asked Benvolio where her son, Romeo, was. Benvolio said that he had seen him before dawn, wandering in a wood at the edge of the city. Lord Montague added that Romeo often spent the night there, crying and sighing, then locked himself in his room all day.

Later Romeo himself told Benvolio why he was behaving so strangely. He was in love with a woman called Rosaline, but it was hopeless because she would have nothing to do with him.

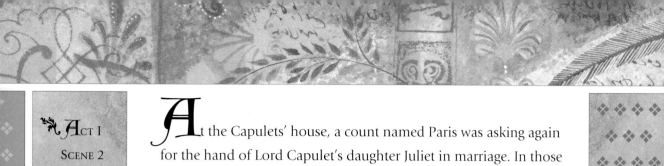

At the Capulets' house, a count named Paris was asking again for the hand of Lord Capulet's daughter Juliet in marriage. In those days the marriages in rich, top-ranking families were arranged, and the daughter's father usually had the final say in who she would marry. A good "match," as it was called, was when a young woman married a man from a family richer and more important than her own. Paris was related to the Prince, so his family was better off than Capulet's. Lord Capulet approved of the match but wanted to wait until Juliet was a little older. He told Paris:

> My child is yet a stranger in the world,
> She hath not seen the change of fourteen years.
> Let two more summers wither in their pride
> Ere we may think her ripe to be a bride.

Younger than she are happy mothers made, Paris protested. But all Lord Capulet's other children had died, so Juliet was very precious to him. He encouraged Paris to take things slowly:

> Earth hath swallow'd all my hopes but she. . . .
> But woo her, gentle Paris, get her heart,
> My will to her consent is but a part.

That night Capulet was going to hold a great feast, a masked ball, at his house. He invited Paris, then sent a servant out into Verona to ask yet more people to the party.

wither: *die*

❖15❖

In the street, the servant met Benvolio and Romeo and invited them to the feast — so long as they were not Montagues! Benvolio said they should go. Rosaline would be there, and, seeing her among other beautiful women, Romeo might feel differently about her:

Compare her face with some that I shall show
And I will make thee think thy swan a crow.

Act I
Scene 3

Back at the house, Lady Capulet was telling Juliet and her old nanny, the Nurse, about Paris. She made it clear that he was a good match — rich, handsome, and well connected — and told Juliet that he would be at the masked ball that night.

Act I
Scene 4

That evening Benvolio and his friend Mercutio, a cousin to the Prince, were fooling around in the street on their way to the feast. Romeo, though, was still lovesick. **I dreamt a dream tonight,** he sighed.

(M)ercutio, always one with a stream of words and wit at the ready, said:

O then I see Queen Mab hath been with you.
She is the fairies' midwife, and she comes
In shape no bigger than an agate stone
On the forefinger of an alderman.

agate: *semiprecious stone*
alderman: *town councilor*

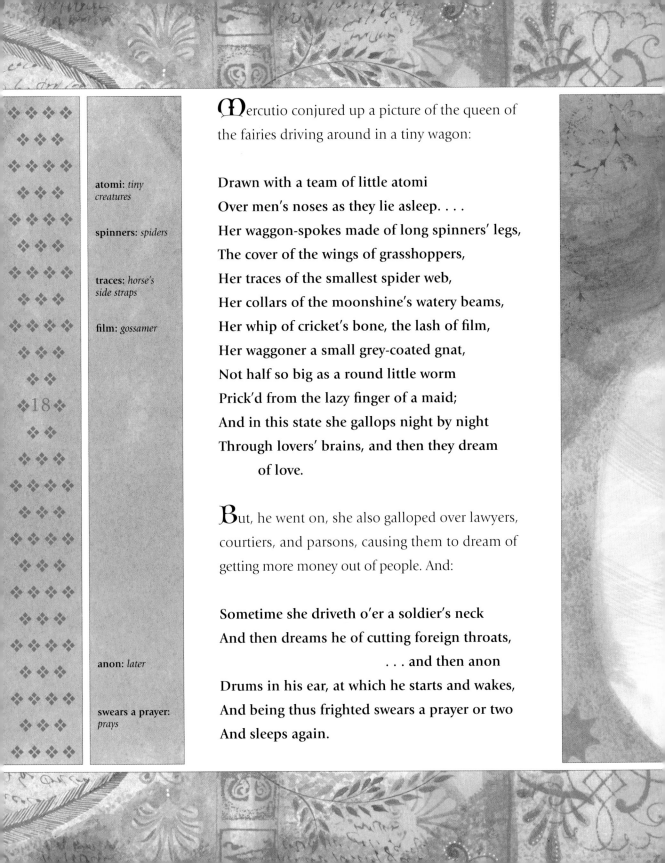

ercutio conjured up a picture of the queen of the fairies driving around in a tiny wagon:

Drawn with a team of little atomi
Over men's noses as they lie asleep. . . .
Her waggon-spokes made of long spinners' legs,
The cover of the wings of grasshoppers,
Her traces of the smallest spider web,
Her collars of the moonshine's watery beams,
Her whip of cricket's bone, the lash of film,
Her waggoner a small grey-coated gnat,
Not half so big as a round little worm
Prick'd from the lazy finger of a maid;
And in this state she gallops night by night
Through lovers' brains, and then they dream
     of love.

But, he went on, she also galloped over lawyers, courtiers, and parsons, causing them to dream of getting more money out of people. And:

Sometime she driveth o'er a soldier's neck
And then dreams he of cutting foreign throats,
                        . . . and then anon
Drums in his ear, at which he starts and wakes,
And being thus frighted swears a prayer or two
And sleeps again.

atomi: *tiny creatures*

spinners: *spiders*

traces: *horse's side straps*

film: *gossamer*

anon: *later*

swears a prayer: *prays*

❖18❖

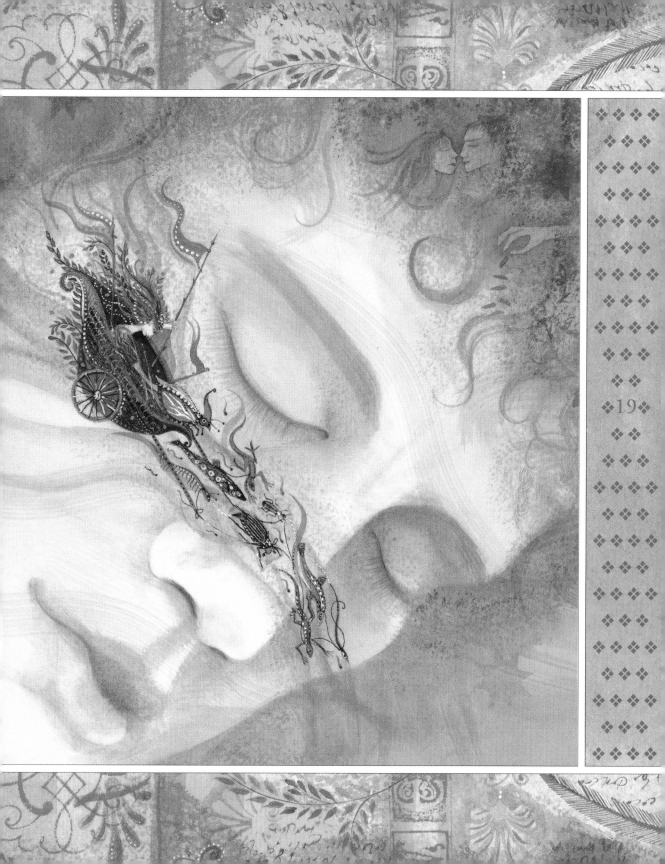

19

Romeo interrupted him. **Peace, peace, Mercutio, peace. Thou talk'st of nothing.**

True, said Mercutio, **I talk of dreams, which are the children of an idle brain.**

As they got near to the Capulets' feast, Romeo became fearful:

. . . my mind misgives
Some consequence yet hanging in the stars
Shall bitterly begin his fearful date
With this night's revels, and expire the term
Of a despised life clos'd in my breast
By some vile forfeit of untimely death.

At the Capulets', the servants were rushing to and fro.

Where's Potpan that he helps not to take away? He shift a trencher! . . . Away with the joint-stools, remove the court-cupboard. . . . You are looked for and called for, asked for and sought for, in the great chamber.

We cannot be here and there too.

❖20❖

consequence:
outcome
his fearful date:
its awful time
revels: *party*
expire: *bring to an end*

ACT I

SCENE 5

trencher: *wooden plate*
court-cupboard:
sideboard

Suddenly, from under his mask, Romeo caught sight of a girl across the room and turned to one of the servants to ask:

What lady's that which doth enrich the hand
Of yonder knight?

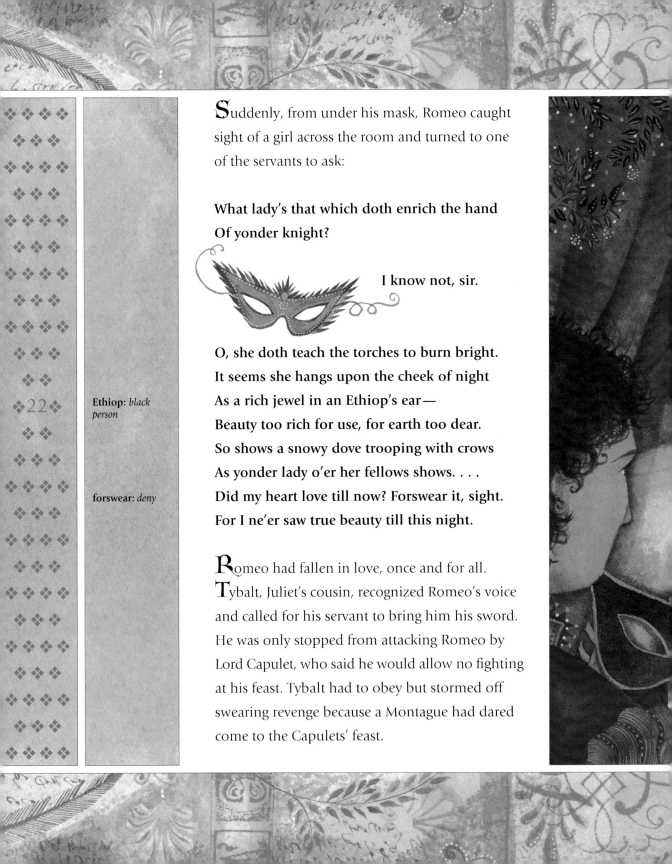

                                    I know not, sir.

O, she doth teach the torches to burn bright.
It seems she hangs upon the cheek of night
As a rich jewel in an Ethiop's ear —
Beauty too rich for use, for earth too dear.
So shows a snowy dove trooping with crows
As yonder lady o'er her fellows shows. . . .
Did my heart love till now? Forswear it, sight.
For I ne'er saw true beauty till this night.

Romeo had fallen in love, once and for all. **T**ybalt, Juliet's cousin, recognized Romeo's voice and called for his servant to bring him his sword. He was only stopped from attacking Romeo by Lord Capulet, who said he would allow no fighting at his feast. Tybalt had to obey but stormed off swearing revenge because a Montague had dared come to the Capulets' feast.

Ethiop: *black person*

forswear: *deny*

22

23

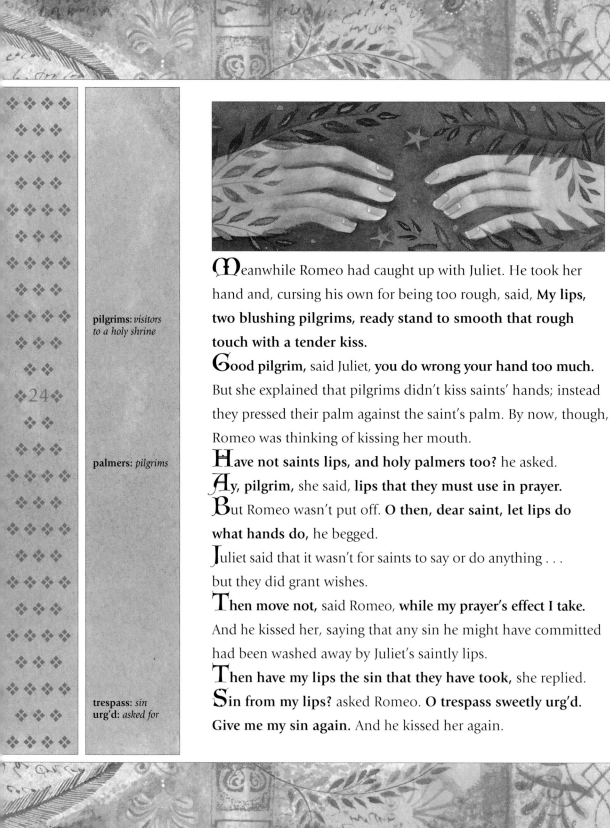

pilgrims: *visitors to a holy shrine*

palmers: *pilgrims*

trespass: *sin*
urg'd: *asked for*

Meanwhile Romeo had caught up with Juliet. He took her hand and, cursing his own for being too rough, said, **My lips, two blushing pilgrims, ready stand to smooth that rough touch with a tender kiss.**

Good pilgrim, said Juliet, **you do wrong your hand too much.** But she explained that pilgrims didn't kiss saints' hands; instead they pressed their palm against the saint's palm. By now, though, Romeo was thinking of kissing her mouth.

Have not saints lips, and holy palmers too? he asked.

Ay, pilgrim, she said, **lips that they must use in prayer.**

But Romeo wasn't put off. **O then, dear saint, let lips do what hands do,** he begged.

Juliet said that it wasn't for saints to say or do anything . . . but they did grant wishes.

Then move not, said Romeo, **while my prayer's effect I take.** And he kissed her, saying that any sin he might have committed had been washed away by Juliet's saintly lips.

Then have my lips the sin that they have took, she replied.

Sin from my lips? asked Romeo. **O trespass sweetly urg'd. Give me my sin again.** And he kissed her again.

But their lovemaking had to stop when the talkative old Nurse came up to them.

Madam, your mother craves a word with you, she said to Juliet.

What is her mother? Romeo asked.

The Nurse replied:

Her mother is the lady of the house,

And a good lady, and a wise and virtuous.

I nurs'd her daughter that you talk'd withal.

I tell you, he that can lay hold of her

Shall have the chinks.

In other words, whoever married Juliet would come in for some big money!

Romeo was left to say to himself:

Is she a Capulet?

O dear account. My life is my foe's debt.

And a moment later he was gone. Juliet, who had also fallen in love once and for all, then asked the Nurse, **What's he that follows here, that would not dance?**

The Nurse replied, **His name is Romeo, and a Montague, the only son of your great enemy.**

And Juliet was left to say to herself:

My only love sprung from my only hate.

craves: begs

withal: with

chinks: money

dear account: great cost
my foe's debt: in my enemy's hands

26

ater that night, Romeo wandered near Lord Capulet's orchard. He couldn't bear to walk past the house, knowing that Juliet was inside: **Can I go forward when my heart is here?** Then he overheard Mercutio — still mocking his lovesickness over Rosaline — and said to himself, **He jests at scars that never felt a wound.**

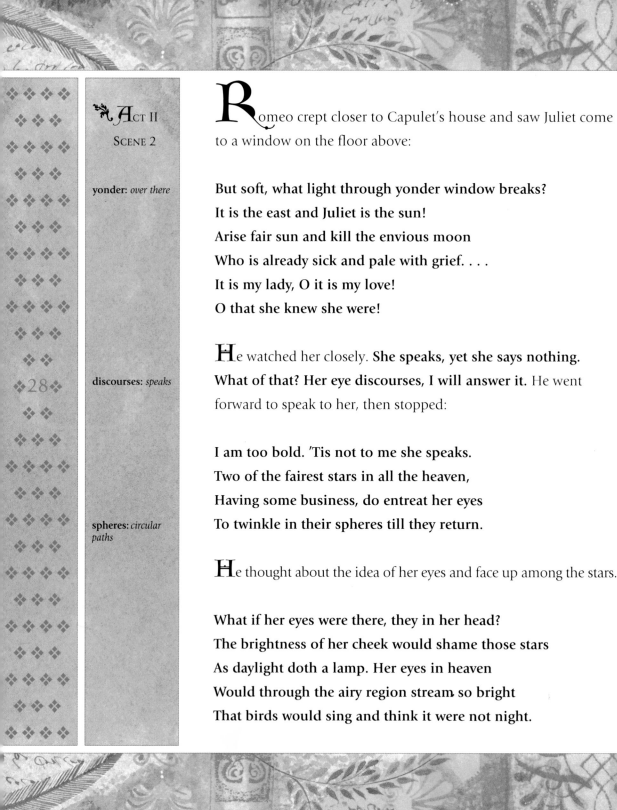

Act II

Scene 2

yonder: over there

discourses: speaks

spheres: circular paths

Romeo crept closer to Capulet's house and saw Juliet come to a window on the floor above:

But soft, what light through yonder window breaks?
It is the east and Juliet is the sun!
Arise fair sun and kill the envious moon
Who is already sick and pale with grief. . . .
It is my lady, O it is my love!
O that she knew she were!

He watched her closely. **She speaks, yet she says nothing. What of that? Her eye discourses, I will answer it.** He went forward to speak to her, then stopped:

I am too bold. 'Tis not to me she speaks.
Two of the fairest stars in all the heaven,
Having some business, do entreat her eyes
To twinkle in their spheres till they return.

He thought about the idea of her eyes and face up among the stars.

What if her eyes were there, they in her head?
The brightness of her cheek would shame those stars
As daylight doth a lamp. Her eyes in heaven
Would through the airy region stream so bright
That birds would sing and think it were not night.

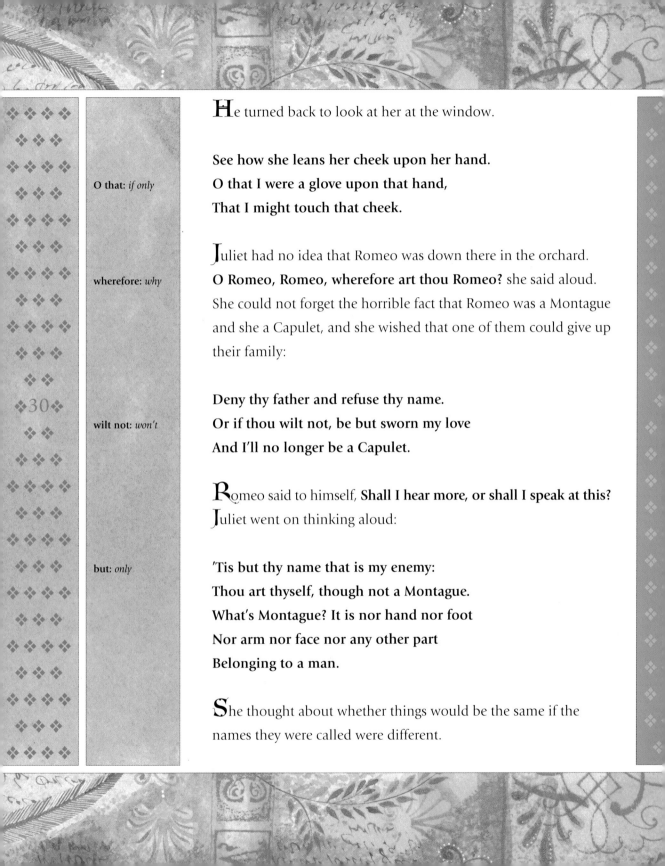

He turned back to look at her at the window.

O that: *if only*

See how she leans her cheek upon her hand.
O that I were a glove upon that hand,
That I might touch that cheek.

Juliet had no idea that Romeo was down there in the orchard.

wherefore: *why*

O Romeo, Romeo, wherefore art thou Romeo? she said aloud.
She could not forget the horrible fact that Romeo was a Montague and she a Capulet, and she wished that one of them could give up their family:

wilt not: *won't*

Deny thy father and refuse thy name.
Or if thou wilt not, be but sworn my love
And I'll no longer be a Capulet.

Romeo said to himself, **Shall I hear more, or shall I speak at this?**
Juliet went on thinking aloud:

but: *only*

'Tis but thy name that is my enemy:
Thou art thyself, though not a Montague.
What's Montague? It is nor hand nor foot
Nor arm nor face nor any other part
Belonging to a man.

She thought about whether things would be the same if the names they were called were different.

retain: *still have*
owes: *owns*
title: *name*
doff: *give up*

What's in a name? That which we call a rose
By any other word would smell as sweet;
So Romeo would, were he not Romeo call'd,
Retain that dear perfection which he owes
Without that title. Romeo, doff thy name,
And for thy name, which is no part of thee,
Take all myself.

Romeo couldn't keep quiet any longer. He called up to her:

> I take thee at thy word.
> Call me but love, and I'll be new baptis'd:
> Henceforth I never will be Romeo.

Juliet was startled and shocked and asked him how he had got there. If one of her family were to find him, he would be killed. Then she realized that he had overheard everything she'd said. She told Romeo that she was too much in love to play games and that she wanted him to be as serious as she was about this love.

> O gentle Romeo,
> If thou dost love, pronounce it faithfully.
> Or, if thou think'st I am too quickly won,
> I'll frown and be perverse and say thee nay.

Romeo began to swear his love in one of his great speeches:

> Lady, by yonder blessed moon I vow,
> That tips with silver all these fruit-tree tops—

But Juliet interrupted him:

> O swear not by the moon, th' inconstant moon,
> That monthly changes in her circled orb,
> Lest that thy love prove likewise variable.

pronounce: *say it*

perverse: *awkward*
nay: *no*

vow: *swear*

inconstant:
changing
orb: *circular path*

lest that: *in case*

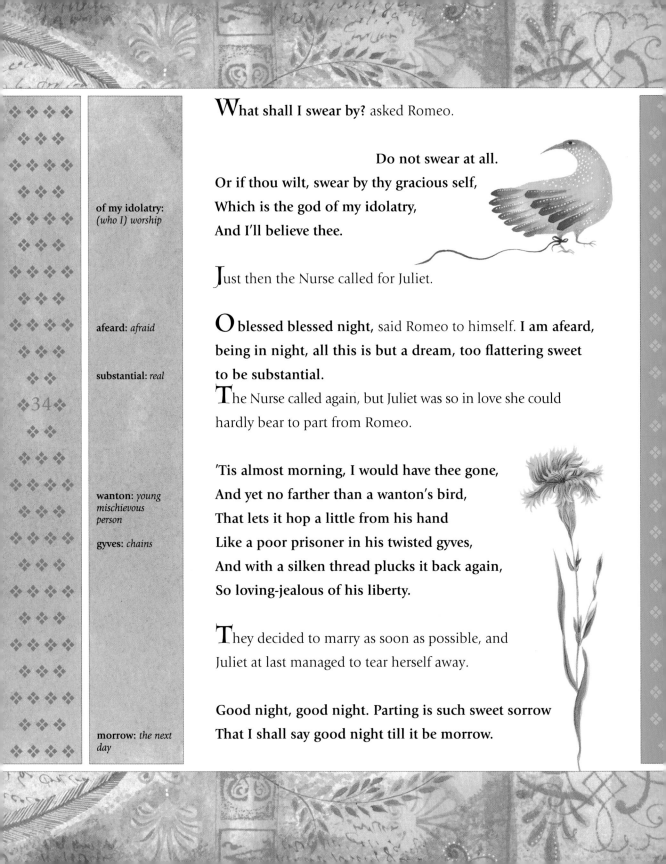

What shall I swear by? asked Romeo.

of my idolatry:
(who I) worship

                              Do not swear at all.
Or if thou wilt, swear by thy gracious self,
Which is the god of my idolatry,
And I'll believe thee.

Just then the Nurse called for Juliet.

afeard: afraid

O blessed blessed night, said Romeo to himself. **I am afeard,**

substantial: real

being in night, all this is but a dream, too flattering sweet
to be substantial.
The Nurse called again, but Juliet was so in love she could
hardly bear to part from Romeo.

❖34❖

'Tis almost morning, I would have thee gone,
And yet no farther than a wanton's bird,
That lets it hop a little from his hand
Like a poor prisoner in his twisted gyves,
And with a silken thread plucks it back again,
So loving-jealous of his liberty.

wanton: young
mischievous
person

gyves: chains

They decided to marry as soon as possible, and
Juliet at last managed to tear herself away.

Good night, good night. Parting is such sweet sorrow
That I shall say good night till it be morrow.

morrow: the next
day

The next day, Romeo visited Friar Laurence, a Franciscan monk, in his cell, a small and sparse room. He asked the friar to carry out a secret marriage ceremony. Though he teased Romeo for forgetting Rosaline so quickly, Friar Laurence agreed. He could see Romeo was serious about Juliet and hoped that the marriage would turn the hatred between the two families to love.

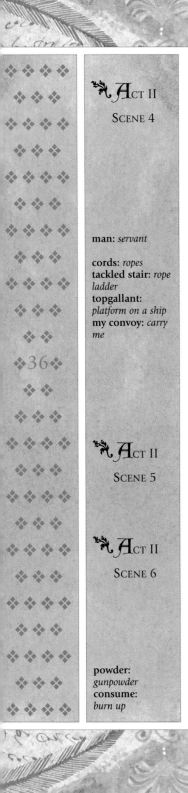

Meanwhile the news on the street was that Tybalt had thrown down a challenge to the Montagues. The Nurse found Romeo, who told her Juliet must come to Friar Laurence's cell that afternoon to be married. He also said he'd thought of a way to spend the night with his new wife:

man: *servant*

cords: *ropes*
tackled stair: *rope ladder*
topgallant: *platform on a ship*
my convoy: *carry me*

Within this hour my man shall be with thee,
And bring thee cords made like a tackled stair,
Which to the high topgallant of my joy
Must be my convoy in the secret night.

As she hurried away, the Nurse warned Romeo that Count Paris also wanted to marry Juliet.

36

Juliet waited impatiently for the Nurse's return. When she finally heard that Romeo had arranged their wedding, she was overjoyed.

Soon after this, Romeo and Juliet met at Friar Laurence's cell and were married, though the friar, seeing how desperately in love they were, said:

powder:
gunpowder
consume:
burn up

These violent delights have violent ends
And in their triumph die, like fire and powder,
Which as they kiss consume.

37

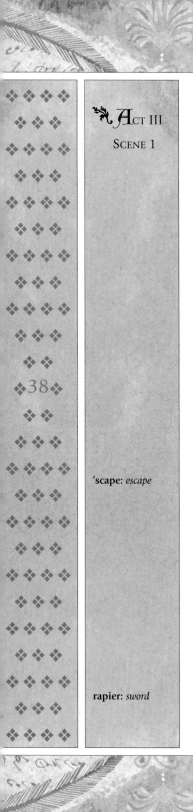
In another part of the city, Mercutio was with a group of young Montagues. Benvolio sensed trouble—the Capulets were around somewhere.

And if we meet, he said, **we shall not 'scape a brawl, for now these hot days is the mad blood stirring.**

Sure enough, Tybalt and his friends turned up, and at once angry words flew between them. Then Romeo appeared on the scene. Tybalt challenged him, but Romeo refused to fight, much to Mercutio's disgust.

T**ybalt, you rat-catcher, will you walk?** shouted Mercutio, challenging Tybalt himself.

I **am for you,** cried Tybalt.

G**entle Mercutio,** said Romeo, **put thy rapier up.** But he couldn't stop them, and soon they were fighting to the death.

'scape: *escape*

rapier: *sword*

38

Romeo was beside himself. **Hold, Tybalt! Good Mercutio!** He ran between them, but Tybalt lunged forward and stabbed Mercutio.

What, art thou hurt? Benvolio asked him.

Ay, ay, a scratch, a scratch, said Mercutio. **Marry, 'tis enough. Where is my page? Go villain, fetch a surgeon.**

Courage, man, the hurt cannot be much, said Romeo.

No, said Mercutio, pretending to agree, **'tis not so deep as a well, nor so wide as a church door, but 'tis enough, 'twill serve.** And, still joking even as he was dying, he said, **Ask for me tomorrow and you shall find me a grave man.** He cursed both the Montagues and the Capulets: **A plague o' both your houses.** Then he turned on Romeo. **Why the devil came you between us? I was hurt under your arm.**

I thought all for the best, said Romeo helplessly.

A few moments later, Mercutio died.

Romeo was now in a terrible position: Tybalt was Juliet's cousin. So by marrying Juliet, he had become Tybalt's cousin only an hour earlier. But Tybalt had just killed one of his dearest friends. Moments later, when Tybalt came back and drew his sword on Romeo, they fought, and this time it was Tybalt who was killed.

Benvolio was appalled:

Romeo, away, be gone,
The citizens are up, and Tybalt slain!
Stand not amaz'd. The Prince will doom thee death
If thou art taken. Hence, be gone, away!

o': *on*

❖40❖

slain: *killed*

taken: *captured*

Romeo rushed off, leaving Benvolio to explain what had happened—to the noble citizens of Verona, to Lord and Lady Montague, Lord and Lady Capulet, and to the Prince himself. The Prince responded immediately. He sent Romeo into exile and laid a huge fine on the Capulets. If Romeo ever came back to Verona, he would be executed.

Act III

Scene 2

In Lord Capulet's orchard, Juliet was pacing to and fro, looking forward to a secret first night of marriage.

Come night, come Romeo, come thou day in night,
For thou wilt lie upon the wings of night
Whiter than new snow upon a raven's back.
Come gentle night, come loving black-brow'd night,
Give me my Romeo; and when I shall die
Take him and cut him out in little stars,
And he will make the face of heaven so fine
That all the world will be in love with night,
And pay no worship to the garish sun.

garish: *bright*

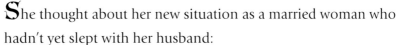

She thought about her new situation as a married woman who hadn't yet slept with her husband:

O, I have bought the mansion of a love
But not possess'd it, and though I am sold,
Not yet enjoy'd. So tedious is this day
As is the night before some festival
To an impatient child that hath new robes
And may not wear them.

The Nurse appeared with the rope ladder, but Juliet saw right away that something was wrong. Had Romeo been hurt? **I saw the wound,** the Nurse said, **I saw it with mine eyes.** But then she cried out, **O Tybalt, Tybalt, the best friend I had.** Were Romeo and Tybalt both dead? Poor Juliet was terrified.

mansion: *house*

possess'd: *owned*

banished: *exiled*

sound: *express*

At last the Nurse managed to explain: **Tybalt is gone and Romeo banished. Romeo that kill'd him, he is banished.** And in her grief, she cursed Romeo for what he'd done:

> **There's no trust,**
> **No faith, no honesty in men. . . .**
> **These griefs, these woes, these sorrows make me old.**
> **Shame come to Romeo.**

Juliet was angry. **Blister'd be thy tongue for such a wish,** she retorted.

The Nurse replied quickly, **Will you speak well of him that kill'd your cousin?**

Shall I speak ill of him that is my husband? answered Juliet. Slowly she began to take everything in. **My husband lives, that Tybalt would have slain, and Tybalt's dead, that would have slain my husband.**

And wasn't there something else? **But O, it presses to my memory. . . . Tybalt is dead and Romeo banished. That "banished," that one word "banished," hath slain ten thousand Tybalts.** Tybalt's death was sad enough, if it had ended there, but Romeo banished as well? **There is no end, no limit, measure, bound, in that word's death. No words can that woe sound.**

The Nurse said she would go out to fetch Romeo to comfort her.

O find him, said Juliet, **give this ring to my true knight and bid him come to take his last farewell.**

Romeo was hiding in Friar Laurence's cell when the friar told him of his banishment. He was grief-stricken. There was nothing outside Verona, he said, except **purgatory, torture, hell itself**. Friar Laurence was shocked and said that Romeo should be thankful the Prince hadn't ordered his death.

Not long after, the Nurse arrived to find Romeo crying. He wondered if Juliet now thought of him as a murderer, and when he was told she was weeping too, he drew his dagger as if to stab himself. Between them, the Nurse and Friar Laurence quieted him down and persuaded him to agree to a plan.

decreed: *ordered*
ascend: *go up to*

Go, get thee to thy love as was decreed, ascend her chamber—hence, and comfort her, ordered the friar. Then he warned Romeo to leave Juliet before dawn and make his way to the nearby city of Mantua until such time as the friar could announce the marriage and beg the Prince's pardon. Even in his despair, Romeo agreed that this was the best thing to do.

In Capulet's house, Lord and Lady Capulet were talking to Paris, who was impatient to marry Juliet. With the family grieving over Tybalt's death, Capulet decided the wedding should happen quickly and told his wife to break the news to Juliet. **I think she will be rul'd in all respects by me,** he said.

45

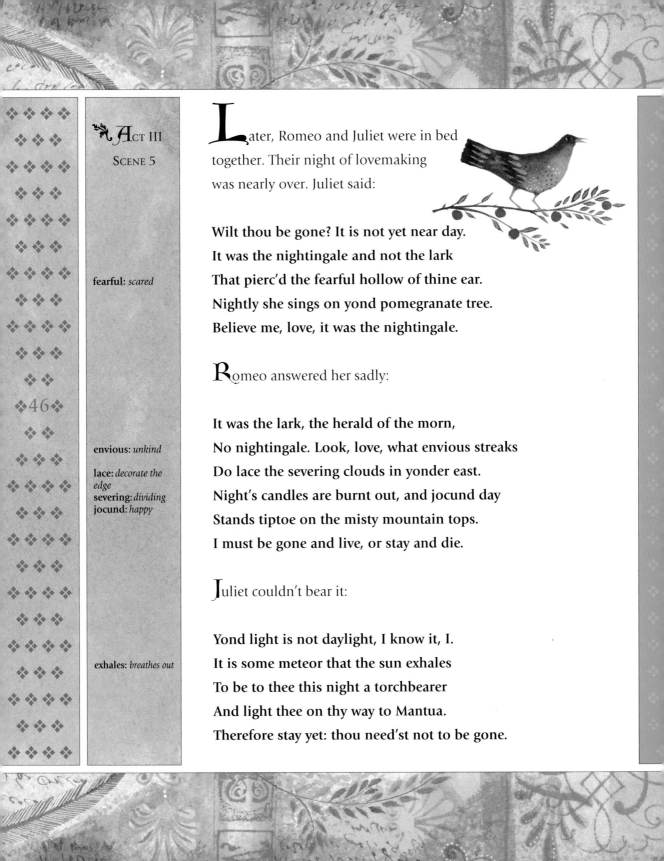

Later, Romeo and Juliet were in bed together. Their night of lovemaking was nearly over. Juliet said:

fearful: *scared*

Wilt thou be gone? It is not yet near day.
It was the nightingale and not the lark
That pierc'd the fearful hollow of thine ear.
Nightly she sings on yond pomegranate tree.
Believe me, love, it was the nightingale.

Romeo answered her sadly:

envious: *unkind*

lace: *decorate the edge*
severing: *dividing*
jocund: *happy*

It was the lark, the herald of the morn,
No nightingale. Look, love, what envious streaks
Do lace the severing clouds in yonder east.
Night's candles are burnt out, and jocund day
Stands tiptoe on the misty mountain tops.
I must be gone and live, or stay and die.

Juliet couldn't bear it:

exhales: *breathes out*

Yond light is not daylight, I know it, I.
It is some meteor that the sun exhales
To be to thee this night a torchbearer
And light thee on thy way to Mantua.
Therefore stay yet: thou need'st not to be gone.

And Romeo pretended to agree that yes, the gray in the sky was not morning: **Come death, and welcome. Juliet wills it so. . . . Let's talk. It is not day.**

It is, it is, said Juliet anxiously. **O now be gone, more light and light it grows.**

More light and light: more dark and dark our woes, Romeo answered sadly.

As he slipped out of the orchard, Juliet's mother entered her bedchamber.

woes: *troubles*

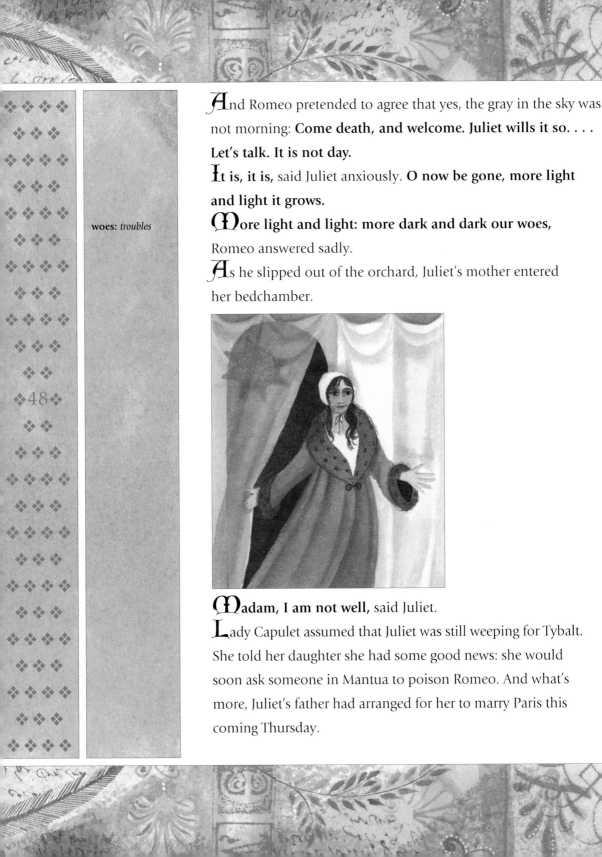

Madam, I am not well, said Juliet.

Lady Capulet assumed that Juliet was still weeping for Tybalt. She told her daughter she had some good news: she would soon ask someone in Mantua to poison Romeo. And what's more, Juliet's father had arranged for her to marry Paris this coming Thursday.

pray: *beg*

Juliet couldn't hide her dismay. **I pray you tell my lord and father, madam, I will not marry yet.** Then she blurted out, **And when I do, I swear it shall be Romeo.** Realizing that she had said too much, she quickly added, **whom you know I hate, rather than Paris.**

Lord Capulet, hearing from his wife that Juliet refused to marry Paris, commanded his daughter to obey, or he would drag her to the church as a traitor is dragged off to be executed.

Disobedient wretch! he spat. Then he turned to Lady Capulet and exclaimed:

> Wife, we scarce thought us blest
> That God had lent us but this only child;
> But now I see this one is one too much,
> And that we have a curse in having her.

Then he worked himself up into a massive rage:

> God's bread, it makes me mad! Day, night, work, play,
> Alone, in company, still my care hath been
> To have her match'd. And having now provided
> A gentleman of noble parentage,
> Of fair demesnes, youthful and nobly lign'd,
> Stuff'd, as they say, with honourable parts,
> Proportion'd as one's thought would wish a man—
> And then to have a wretched puling fool,
> A whining mammet, in her fortune's tender,
> To answer "I'll not wed, I cannot love,
> I am too young, I pray you pardon me!"

He threatened Juliet again:

> Graze where you will, you shall not house with me. . . .
> And you be mine I'll give you to my friend;
> And you be not, hang! Beg! Starve! Die in the streets!

fair demesnes: *fine property*
nobly lign'd: *well connected*

puling: *crying*

mammet: *puppet*
in her fortune's tender: *in her good fortune*

graze: *feed*
house: *live*
and: *if*

With that, he stormed out.

There was no kindness from Lady Capulet either. Now Juliet had only one person left to turn to. **What sayst thou? Hast thou not a word of joy? Some comfort, Nurse,** she begged.

But the Nurse suggested that Juliet should think again about marrying Paris. **O, he's a lovely gentleman. Romeo's a dishclout to him.**

Juliet realized that everyone had turned against her. She cursed the Nurse, calling her **ancient damnation** and **wicked fiend.** Then she decided to go and see Friar Laurence to find some way out of her terrible situation. **If all else fail, myself have power to die.** She would, if necessary, kill herself.

Act IV

Scene 1

Juliet arrived just as Count Paris was asking the friar to perform their wedding ceremony on Thursday.

Happily met, my lady and my wife, Paris said delightedly.

The friar managed to get rid of him, and Juliet poured out her feelings. **I long to die,** she said with a knife in her hand, **if what thou speak'st speak not of remedy.**

remedy: *help*

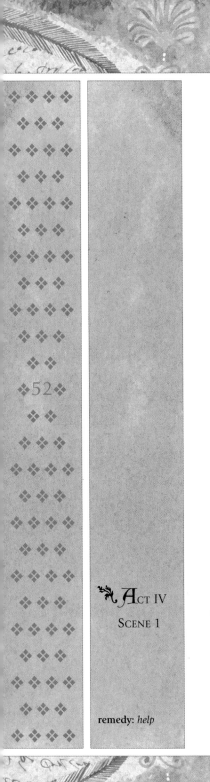

Hold, daughter, the friar said. **I do spy a kind of hope.**
He saw in her the strength of will to undertake something
very difficult and dangerous.

Juliet's answer was a cry of hope mixed with despair:

O, bid me leap, rather than marry Paris,
From off the battlements of any tower,
Or walk in thievish ways, or bid me lurk
Where serpents are. Chain me with roaring bears,
Or hide me nightly in a charnel-house
O'ercover'd quite with dead men's rattling bones,
With reeky shanks and yellow chapless skulls.
Or bid me go into a new-made grave,
And hide me with a dead man in his shroud —
Things that, to hear them told, have made me tremble —
And I will do it without fear or doubt,
To live an unstain'd wife to my sweet love.

Seeing how real and strong Juliet's feelings were, the friar put
his plan to her. She must go home and pretend to be happy about
marrying Paris. On the night before the wedding she must not let
the Nurse sleep in her chamber. Then she must drink a liquor
from a little glass vial he would give her. The liquor would flow
through her veins, stop her pulse, and make it look as if she
were dead.

But what would happen then?

charnel-house: *storage place for skeletons*
quite: *completely*
reeky shanks: *smelly shinbones*
chapless: *jawless*

shroud: *burial sheet*

unstain'd: *innocent*

53

Her bridegroom, Paris, would find her lifeless body, and she would be buried in the Capulet family tomb. **Two and forty hours** later she would wake up. In the meantime, the friar would send letters to Romeo, who would come and take her to Mantua.

Hearing this, Juliet eagerly reached for the vial.

Give me, give me! O tell not me of fear.

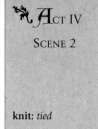 **A**CT IV
SCENE 2

knit: *tied*

wayward: *naughty*
reclaim'd: *won back*

Meanwhile Lord Capulet was preparing for the wedding. He had just commanded that twenty skillful cooks be hired when Juliet came home saying she was sorry for being disobedient. Her father was pleased.

I'll have this knot knit up tomorrow morning, he said, moving the wedding forward a day. **My heart is wondrous light since this same wayward girl is so reclaim'd.**

Later that night, Juliet sent the Nurse away from her bedchamber. Once she was alone, she thought of all the things that could go wrong with Friar Laurence's plan:

I have a faint cold fear thrills through my veins
That almost freezes up the heat of life. . . .
How if, when I am laid into the tomb,
I wake before the time that Romeo
Come to redeem me? There's a fearful point!
Shall I not then be stifled in the vault,
To whose foul mouth no healthsome air breathes in,
And there die strangled ere my Romeo comes? . . .
Where for this many hundred years the bones
Of all my buried ancestors are pack'd,
Where bloody Tybalt yet but green in earth
Lies festering in his shroud . . .

This horrifying picture of the Capulet family tomb led her to think of even worse possibilities:

O, if I wake, shall I not be distraught,
Environed with all these hideous fears,
And madly play with my forefathers' joints,
And pluck the mangled Tybalt from his shroud,
And, in this rage, with some great kinsman's bone
As with a club dash out my desperate brains?

redeem: *save*

vault: *tomb*

❖56❖

green in earth:
freshly buried
festering: *rotting*

environed:
surrounded by

Then she had a ghastly vision of her dead cousin Tybalt:

O look, methinks I see my cousin's ghost
Seeking out Romeo that did spit his body
Upon a rapier's point! Stay, Tybalt, stay!
Romeo, Romeo, Romeo, here's drink! I drink to thee!

She drank the liquor from the vial and fell upon her bed.

The next morning, everyone was up early in the Capulet household. Lady Capulet was running about making sure there were enough spices; the Nurse said they needed more dates and quinces in the kitchen. **Look to the bak'd meats,** Lord Capulet ordered. **Spare not for cost.** The servants rushed through, carrying logs, baskets, and spits to roast the meat on. Then Paris arrived, accompanied by musicians.

Go waken Juliet, Lord Capulet ordered the Nurse.
Make haste! The bridegroom he is come already.
Make haste I say.

Aᴄᴛ IV
Sᴄᴇɴᴇ 5

untimely: out of season

Up in Juliet's chamber, the Nurse was trying to wake her as she did every morning. But Juliet didn't stir. Suddenly the Nurse screamed, realizing she was dead. **L**ord and Lady Capulet rushed in and were overwhelmed with grief.

My child, my only life,
cried Lady Capulet.

Death lies on her like an untimely frost
Upon the sweetest flower of all the field,
said Lord Capulet.

Friar Laurence and Paris arrived and were told the terrible news. Like the good Christian that he was, the friar tried to calm everyone by reassuring them that Juliet was now in heaven. Miserably, Lord Capulet realized that the wedding feast had to turn into a funeral:

instruments:
musical instruments

sullen dirges:
sad songs
corse: *corpse*

Our instruments to melancholy bells,
Our wedding cheer to a sad burial feast;
Our solemn hymns to sullen dirges change,
Our bridal flowers serve for a buried corse,
And all things change them to the contrary.

Meanwhile, Romeo was walking down a street in Mantua, certain that joyful news was at hand. He'd dreamt that Juliet had come and found him dead but then breathed life into him by kissing his lips.

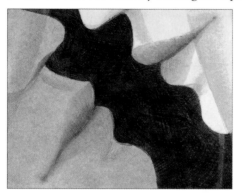

Suddenly Balthasar, his servant, rushed up with terrible news: Juliet was dead and in the Capulet family tomb.

Then I defy you, stars! cried Romeo. He knew immediately what to do: he would go to Juliet's tomb and kill himself and join her in heaven.

Romeo ordered Balthasar to prepare horses for the journey to Verona. He decided that he would kill himself with poison bought from an old apothecary he remembered seeing, a seller of drugs and potions.

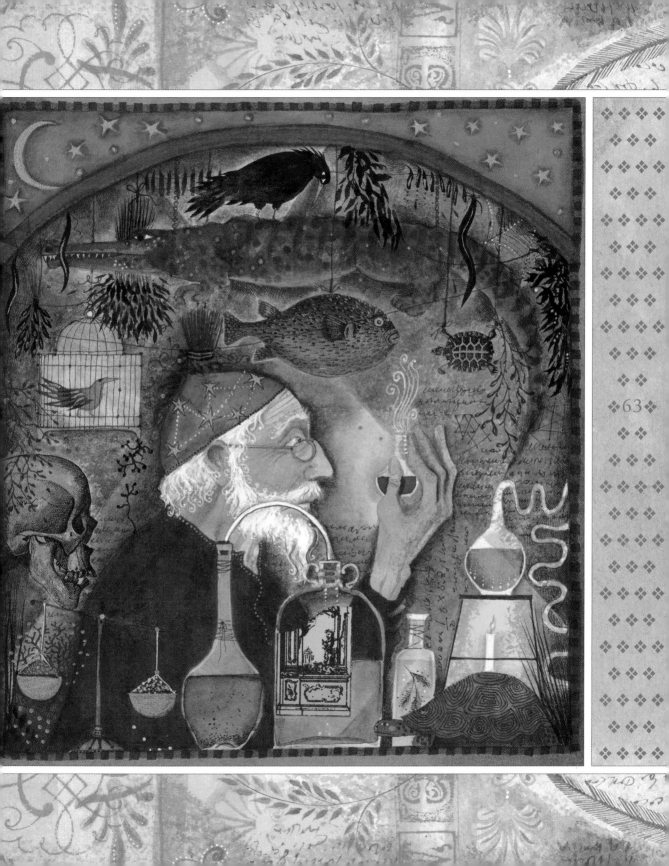

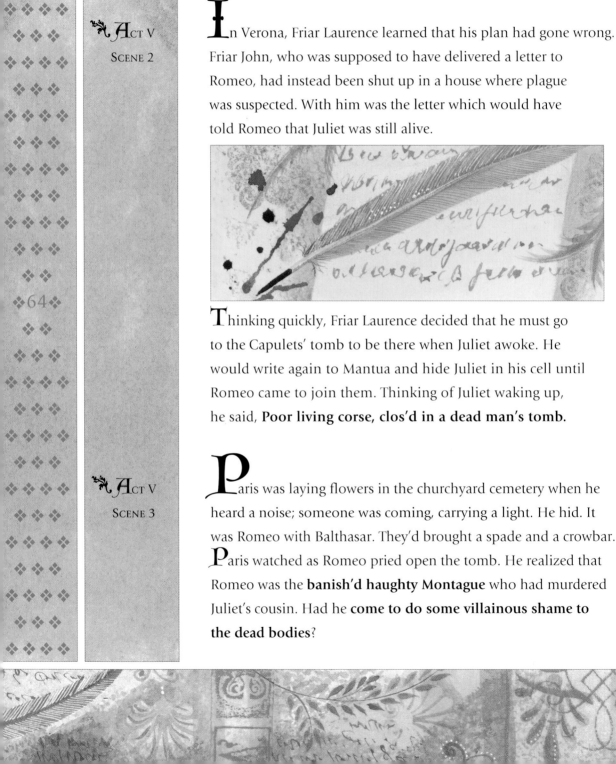
In Verona, Friar Laurence learned that his plan had gone wrong. Friar John, who was supposed to have delivered a letter to Romeo, had instead been shut up in a house where plague was suspected. With him was the letter which would have told Romeo that Juliet was still alive.

Thinking quickly, Friar Laurence decided that he must go to the Capulets' tomb to be there when Juliet awoke. He would write again to Mantua and hide Juliet in his cell until Romeo came to join them. Thinking of Juliet waking up, he said, **Poor living corse, clos'd in a dead man's tomb.**

Paris was laying flowers in the churchyard cemetery when he heard a noise; someone was coming, carrying a light. He hid. It was Romeo with Balthasar. They'd brought a spade and a crowbar. Paris watched as Romeo pried open the tomb. He realized that Romeo was the **banish'd haughty Montague** who had murdered Juliet's cousin. Had he **come to do some villainous shame to the dead bodies**?

Stop thy unhallow'd toil, vile Montague, he shouted, threatening Romeo with death.

Good gentle youth, tempt not a desperate man, Romeo replied.

Paris tried to arrest him and in the fight that followed was killed. Romeo laid him in the Capulets' tomb, then prepared to take the poison and die.

How oft when men are at the point of death have they **been merry!** Romeo observed. He looked at Juliet's body.

> O my love, my wife,
> Death that hath suck'd the honey of thy breath
> Hath had no power yet upon thy beauty.
> Thou art not conquer'd. Beauty's ensign yet
> Is crimson in thy lips and in thy cheeks,
> And Death's pale flag is not advanced there.

ensign: *flag*

advanced: *yet to be seen*

He caught sight
of another body and
realized it was Tybalt,
the man he had killed;
and then, talking to Juliet,
he said:

> Here, here, will I remain
> With worms that are thy chambermaids. O here
> Will I set up my everlasting rest
> And shake the yoke of inauspicious stars
> From this world-wearied flesh. Eyes, look your last.
> Arms, take your last embrace!

yoke: *heavy grip*
inauspicious: *unlucky*

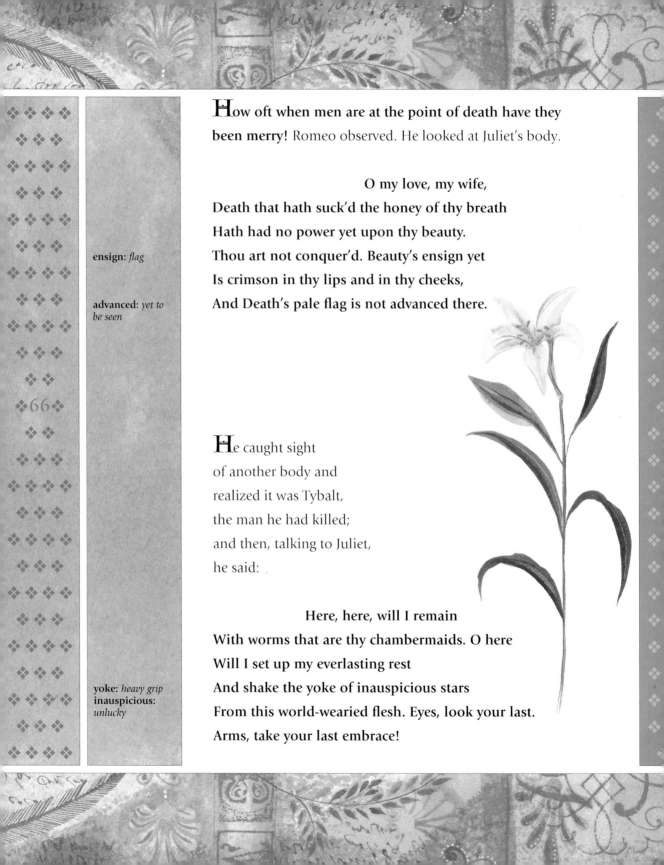

He knelt down and held Juliet's body in his arms.

                              And lips, O you
The doors of breath, seal with a righteous kiss
A dateless bargain to engrossing Death.

He kissed her lips.

Then he poured out the poison into a little cup,
raised the cup, and offered Juliet a toast: **Here's to my**
love! He drank. **O true apothecary, thy drugs are quick.**
Thus with a kiss I die.

And he fell down beside her.

dateless: *timeless*
engrossing:
all-consuming

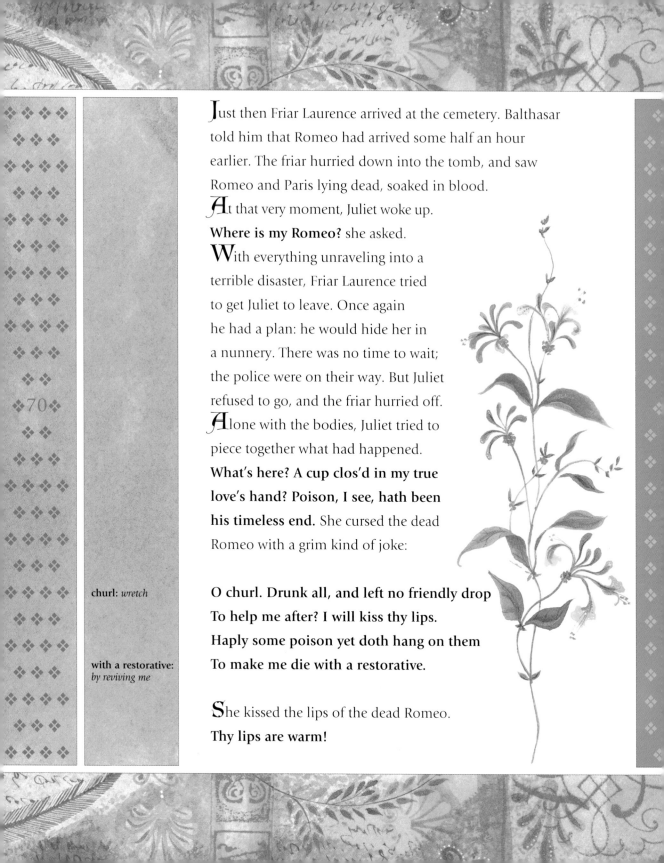

Just then Friar Laurence arrived at the cemetery. Balthasar told him that Romeo had arrived some half an hour earlier. The friar hurried down into the tomb, and saw Romeo and Paris lying dead, soaked in blood.

At that very moment, Juliet woke up.

Where is my Romeo? she asked.

With everything unraveling into a terrible disaster, Friar Laurence tried to get Juliet to leave. Once again he had a plan: he would hide her in a nunnery. There was no time to wait; the police were on their way. But Juliet refused to go, and the friar hurried off.

Alone with the bodies, Juliet tried to piece together what had happened.

What's here? A cup clos'd in my true love's hand? Poison, I see, hath been his timeless end. She cursed the dead Romeo with a grim kind of joke:

70

churl: *wretch*

with a restorative: *by reviving me*

**O churl. Drunk all, and left no friendly drop
To help me after? I will kiss thy lips.
Haply some poison yet doth hang on them
To make me die with a restorative.**

She kissed the lips of the dead Romeo.

Thy lips are warm!

Suddenly she heard noises. Outside, the police were arriving. What could she do? She saw Romeo's dagger. **O happy dagger.** Talking to the blade itself and preparing a place where it could go in, she said, **This is thy sheath. There rust, and let me die.** And she stabbed herself.

Soon everyone—the police, the Capulets, the Montagues, the Prince, and the people of Verona—was at the scene. Friar Laurence told them what had happened and said that he was the one who should stand condemned for the part he had played. But the Prince blamed Lord Capulet and Lord Montague—their hatred for each other had led to this dreadful slaughter.

Lord Capulet turned to his greatest enemy and said, **O brother Montague, give me thy hand.** As they shook hands he said, **This is my daughter's jointure, for no more can I demand.** Friendship was all the settlement he wanted.

jointure: *marriage settlement*

Montague replied by saying:

> But I can give thee more,
> For I will raise her statue in pure gold,
> That whiles Verona by that name is known,
> There shall no figure at such rate be set
> As that of true and faithful Juliet.

Capulet said grimly:

> As rich shall Romeo's by his lady's lie,
> Poor sacrifices of our enmity.

Lord Montague and Lord Capulet embraced each other sadly and so did all the members of the two households while the people of Verona looked on. **T**hen the Prince spoke:

> A glooming peace this morning with it brings:
> The sun for sorrow will not show his head.
> Go hence to have more talk of these sad things.
> Some shall be pardon'd, and some punished,
> For never was a story of more woe
> Than this of Juliet and her Romeo.

figure: *person*
rate: *value*

These were the last words the audience heard in the theatre in Elizabethan London. We'll never know what thoughts filled their minds as they filed out into the streets, returning to all the pleasures and disasters, joys and sadnesses, hopes and fears, securities and dangers of their lives. We might guess that many found people and situations in the story to compare to those they knew or had heard of: stern, powerful rulers; rich families feuding; young lovers madly in love; servants hurrying to do what their masters and mistresses told them; holy men plotting and scheming to make things happen according to what they thought was right; strict fathers demanding that their daughters make a match that suited the family's position in society; and, perhaps—who knows?—a young woman, clever and strong enough to say and do what she wanted.

All that you or I really know is how *we* feel about all those people and the struggles they went through.

One more thing: when you get the chance, go and see the play. That's why plays are written—so that people like you will go and see them. That's why, over four hundred years ago, William Shakespeare wrote

THE MOST EXCELLENT AND LAMENTABLE TRAGEDY
OF ROMEO AND JULIET.

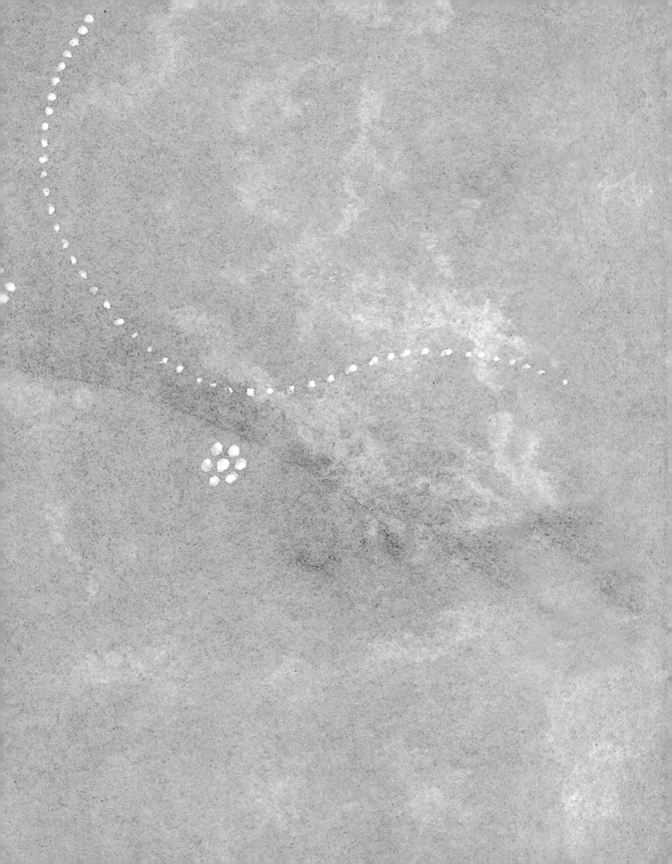